WHERE'S THE MEERKAT?

ILLUSTRATED BY PAUL MORAN,
STEVE WILTSHIRE AND SIMON ECOB

WRITTEN BY JEN WAINWRIGHT

DESIGNED BY ANGIE ALLISON AND ZOE QUAYLE

Michael O'Mara Books Limited

A Meerkat Adventure

Prepare to embark on an adventure that will take you all around the globe. You're about to meet a family of mischievous meerkats who are going on the trip of a lifetime, and have invited you along for the ride.

Your Challenge ...

All you have to do is spot ten meerkats in each picture. Sounds simple, right? Be warned, this family is expert at blending in with a crowd, so you'll need your sharpest searching skills. If you get stuck, the solutions can be found at the back of the book.

Really eagle-eyed searchers can use the special 'Spotter's Checklists' at the back of the book, where there's more fun stuff to find in every picture and tick off.

Bon voyage and happy searching ...

Meet The Family

Now it's time to meet the meerkats and find out more about the crazy critters in this fantastic family.

Lives in:
Sandy Warren, Africa

Likes:
Travel, adventure, mischief, fancy dress

Favourite Music:
The Beetles, MeerKaty Perry

Favourite Films:
An American Meerkat in Paris,
Meerkat On A Hot Tin Roof

Favourite Books:
Termites And Men by John Steinbeck,
The Burrowers by Mary Norton

Favourite quotations:
'You must be the change you want to see in the world' – Meerkatma Gandhi.

Back row (left to right): Miranda, Florian, Albert, Raoul, Sofia, Matthew
Front row (left to right): Frankie, Maxwell, Samson, Hannah.

Individual Profiles

Read on to discover more vital information about each member of the family.

Miranda:

As the maternal figure of the group, Miranda is practical, sensible and never without a clean hanky. She also knows the lyrics to every James Bond theme by heart.

Florian:

This chirpy chappy makes a mean banana milkshake, and has recently started learning folk dancing. He also has an unrivalled back catalogue of mongoose-themed jokes.

Albert:

Albert is mostly known as 'Grampy' to the others in the group. He's a dignified and sprightly old gent with a vast collection of vintage baseball cards.

Raoul:

Raoul dreams of being a rock star. He plays the bassoon (badly), but has written an epic rock ballad, which he hopes will get airtime on *Scorpion FM.*

Sofia:

The highlight of Sofia's life has been her nomination for 'Miss Meerkat' – a prestigious beauty pageant. She point-blank refuses to travel anywhere without her fur straighteners.

Matthew:

Here comes trouble. Matthew can usually be found exactly where he shouldn't be. His special skills include being able to fit six biscuits in his mouth at once.

Frankie:

Frankie's the baby of the bunch. She's also a feisty tomboy, who particularly enjoys infuriating Sofia by hiding her beauty products up trees and in holes.

Maxwell:

Always full of bright ideas, Maxwell has almost perfected his designs for the 'Meerkat-O-Matic' – a device that's part predator alarm, part jet-pack.

Samson:

Samson is a bit of a dark horse. He may be a bookworm with a keen interest in botany, but he's also a karate black belt with a spectacular roundhouse kick.

Hannah:

Hannah is a true artist. She's always painting and sculpting, but her recent series of 'cubist family portraits' has not been greeted with tremendous enthusiasm by her siblings.

Rio De Janeiro, Brazil

The family have landed in Rio and they're ready to party! They are headed straight for the Sambadrome – a huge concrete stadium, where as many as 50,000 musicians and performers parade wearing elaborate costumes in front of cheering crowds.

Hannah and Sofia are excited about dancing the night away, and have been practising their best samba steps. The parties and parades often continue until sunrise, so there will be some sleepy meerkats tomorrow ...

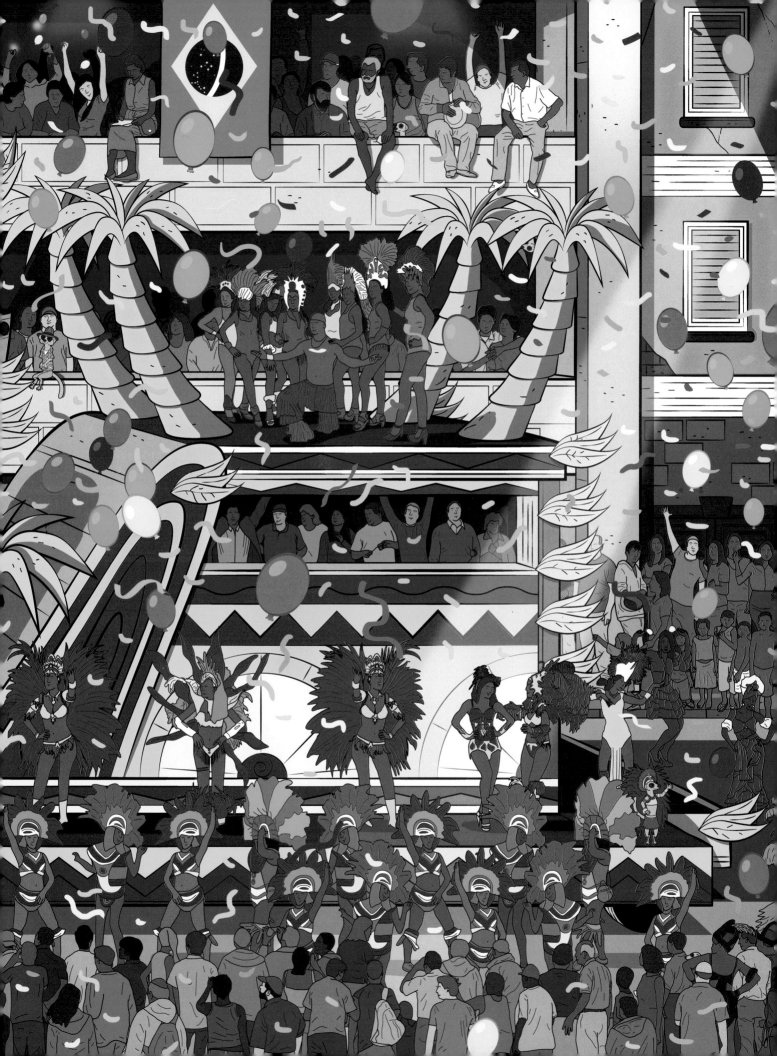

New York, USA

While the grown-ups in the family want to see the Empire State Building and the Statue of Liberty, for Frankie and Raoul it's all about Times Square. They're dazzled by all the cool neon signs, called 'spectaculars'.

1.6 million people pass through Times Square every day, so it's easy to get lost in the crowds. But Frankie and Raoul have promised that they'll meet the others at Toys 'R' Us. With a giant, moving T-Rex, a Ferris wheel and a two-storey dolls' house, it's the place they're most excited about going on this whole trip.

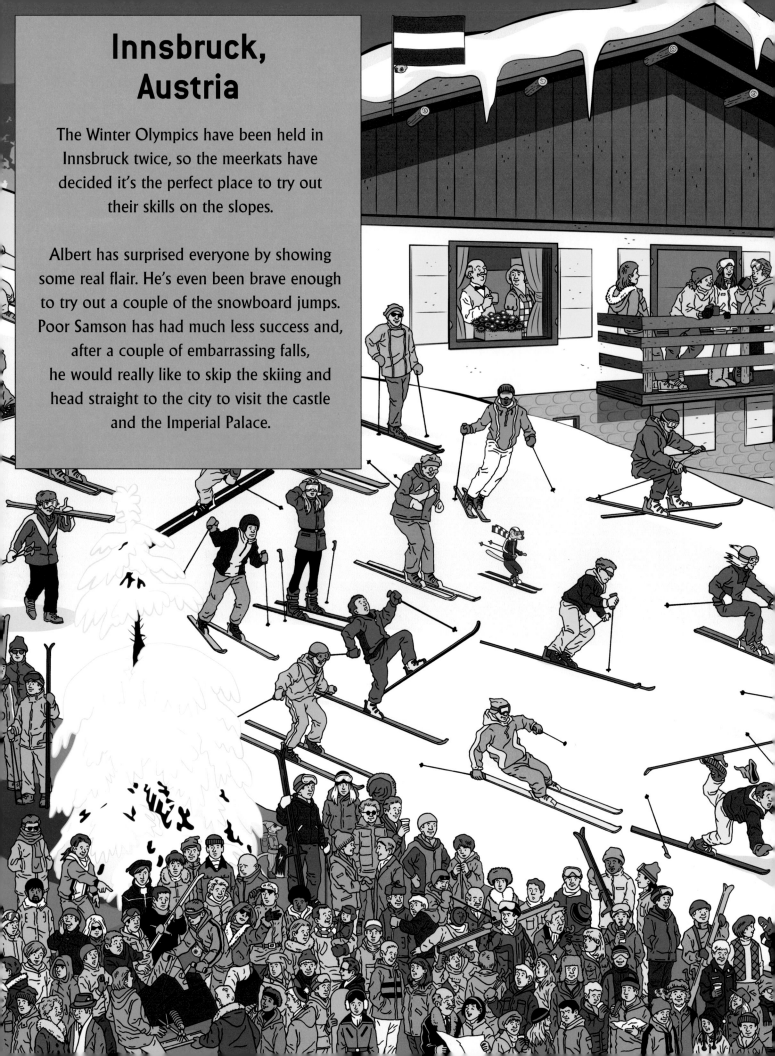

Innsbruck, Austria

The Winter Olympics have been held in Innsbruck twice, so the meerkats have decided it's the perfect place to try out their skills on the slopes.

Albert has surprised everyone by showing some real flair. He's even been brave enough to try out a couple of the snowboard jumps. Poor Samson has had much less success and, after a couple of embarrassing falls, he would really like to skip the skiing and head straight to the city to visit the castle and the Imperial Palace.

Paris, France

Ever since she was a pup, Sofia has dreamed of visiting Paris. She has been driving everyone mad with her constant talk about the shopping, the fashion, the shopping, the romance, the shopping, the pastries, the shopping and ... the shopping.

As well as hitting the chic boutiques along the Champs-Elysées, she plans to climb the Eiffel Tower at night, all 324 metres of it, including the antennae on top – ouch! She wants to see why Paris is known as 'The City of Lights.' Ooh la la!

BOULANGERIE

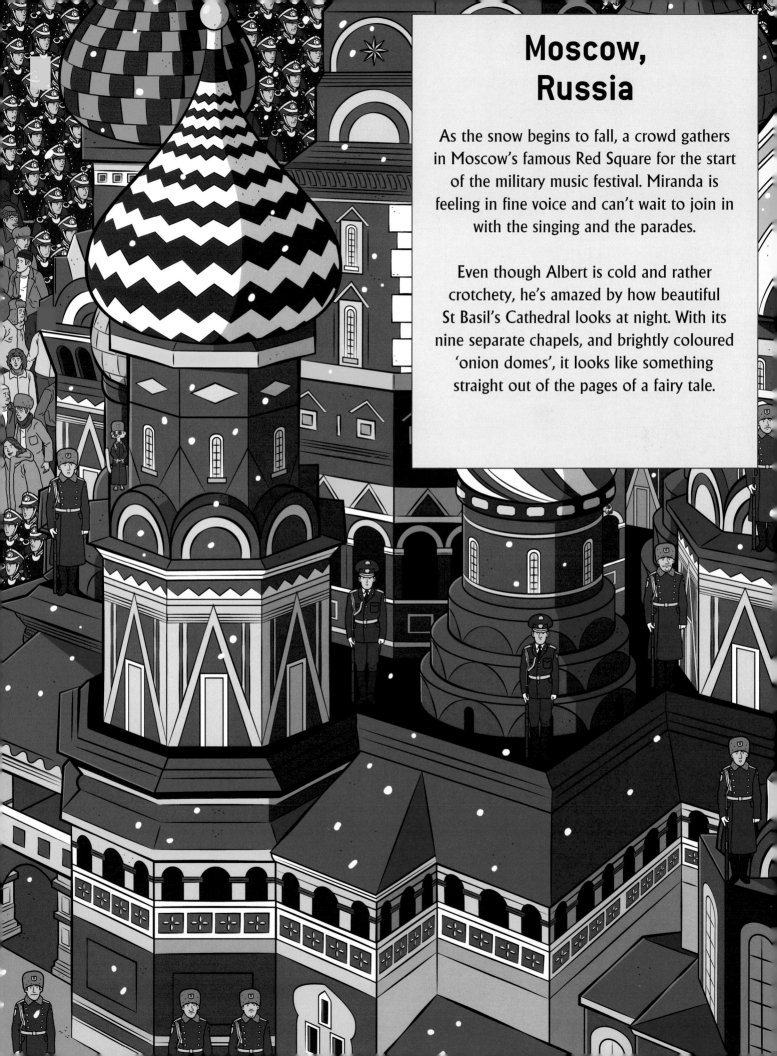

Moscow, Russia

As the snow begins to fall, a crowd gathers in Moscow's famous Red Square for the start of the military music festival. Miranda is feeling in fine voice and can't wait to join in with the singing and the parades.

Even though Albert is cold and rather crotchety, he's amazed by how beautiful St Basil's Cathedral looks at night. With its nine separate chapels, and brightly coloured 'onion domes', it looks like something straight out of the pages of a fairy tale.

The Great Wall, China

The Great Wall of China stretches for a massive 8,851.8 kilometres. Florian's eyes nearly fell out of his head when Albert suggested they tackle all of it!

Hannah loves the legend of Meng Jiang Nu, which tells of a beautiful young woman who cried so much when she heard that her husband had died while building the wall, that a whole section of it came tumbling down. Hannah thinks this is so romantic that she's not even complaining about her paws hurting from all the walking.

Easter Island, South Pacific

Gadget-mad Maxwell was convinced that Easter Island would be 'well boring'. But, actually, he's finding it fascinating – even though there's not much in the way of mobile phone signal.

The giant statues, known as 'Moai', are scattered all over the island, some of them weighing up to about 80 tonnes. Lots of them were carved over 1,000 years ago. Maxwell is busy trying to work out how the enormous objects were moved across the island in the days before machinery was used.

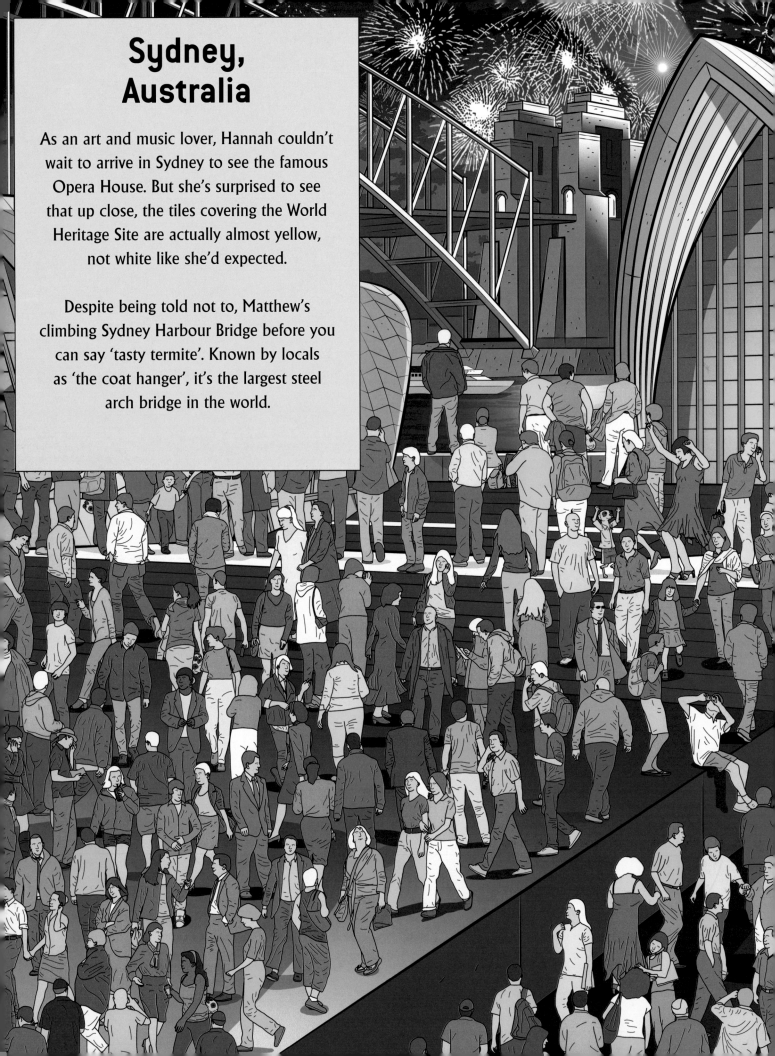

Sydney, Australia

As an art and music lover, Hannah couldn't wait to arrive in Sydney to see the famous Opera House. But she's surprised to see that up close, the tiles covering the World Heritage Site are actually almost yellow, not white like she'd expected.

Despite being told not to, Matthew's climbing Sydney Harbour Bridge before you can say 'tasty termite'. Known by locals as 'the coat hanger', it's the largest steel arch bridge in the world.

London, UK

Florian has fallen in love with London in the short time that the family have been here. He has bought an enormous Union Jack flag, and some commemorative Royal Wedding plates and mugs showing Prince William and Catherine, Duchess of Cambridge, to decorate the warren back at home.

Today, it's the changing of the guard at Buckingham Palace, and the crowds have gathered to watch the soldiers marching in their uniforms and tall bearskin hats.

Venice, Italy

When it's Carnival time in Venice, the streets and canals come alive. Everywhere you look there are musicians, jugglers and revellers wearing elaborate and beautiful masks.

After having created his very own pizza, with all the toppings that the restaurant could manage to find, Matthew has now decided to try his hand as a gondolier, using a pole to push the sleek, black boats along the canals. Let's hope he doesn't get 'canal-sick'!

Giza, Egypt

The Great Sphinx of Giza is a truly impressive sight. The enormous statue has the body of a lion, and the head of a man, although Raoul thinks it would look much better with the body of a dragon and the head of a meerkat.

Raoul has learned that the Ancient Egyptians would mummify their dead by wrapping them in bandages. Before this could happen, they removed the dead person's brain through their nose. He is now threatening to do this to his sisters whenever they annoy him, which is most of the time.

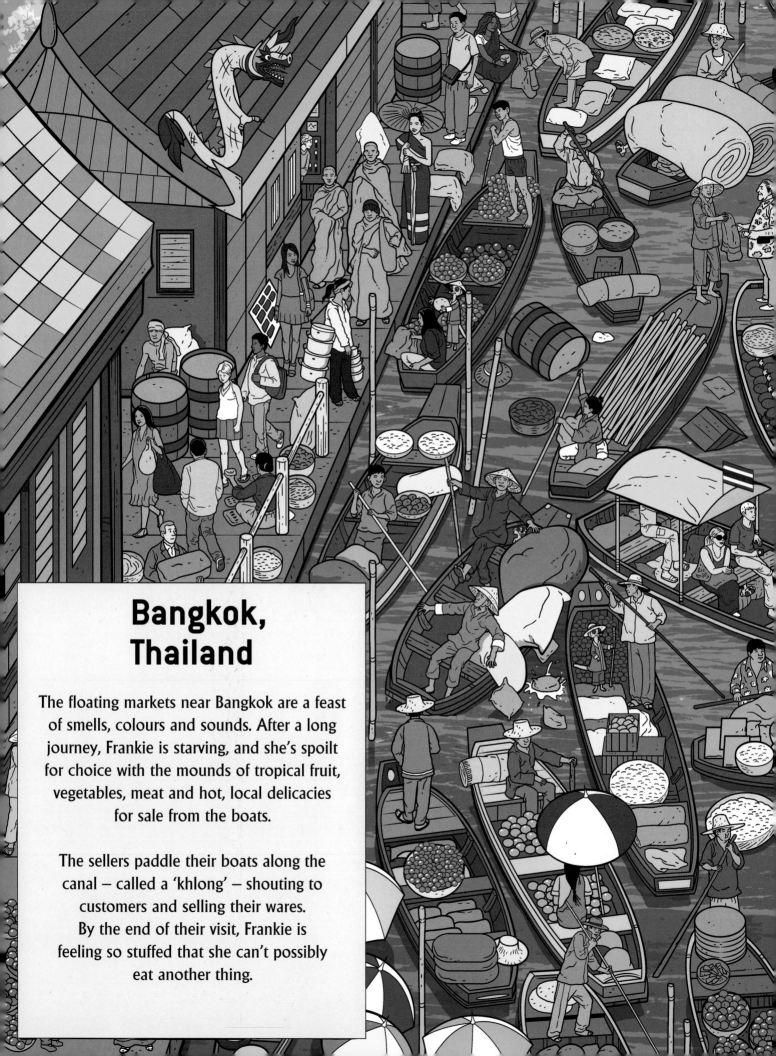

Bangkok, Thailand

The floating markets near Bangkok are a feast of smells, colours and sounds. After a long journey, Frankie is starving, and she's spoilt for choice with the mounds of tropical fruit, vegetables, meat and hot, local delicacies for sale from the boats.

The sellers paddle their boats along the canal – called a 'khlong' – shouting to customers and selling their wares. By the end of their visit, Frankie is feeling so stuffed that she can't possibly eat another thing.

Kyoto, Japan

Miranda has been quietly looking forward to this visit for ages. The Shinto shrines of Japan are known as places of calm and tranquility, and she can't wait to take some deep breaths and absorb some of the peace and quiet among the blossoming cherry trees.

The beautiful building is a shrine to the 'kami' – the sacred spirits of the Shinto religion. Kami aren't always gods and goddesses, they can also be forces of nature, such as thunder and tornados, or parts of the natural world, such as lakes and trees.

Santa Cruz, USA

The meerkats have decided to relax for a while on the beach at Santa Cruz in the warm California sun. While Sofia struts her stuff on the boardwalk, Raoul is having a go at surfing, with hilariously mixed results.

Later, the family plan to go to the funfair. Hannah and Samson can't wait to go on the Giant Dipper, the iconic wooden roller coaster that opened in 1924, but Albert has decided he's getting too old for this sort of thing. He'll sit back and watch the youngsters while tucking in to some sugary funnel cake – a fairground specialty.

The Great Barrier Reef, Australia

In the crystal-clear waters of the Great Barrier Reef, there are more than 400 different types of coral in beautiful colours. Samson is in heaven – his mum says he's always been a water baby and he's having a whale of a time swimming with the fish and sea turtles.

Even though the reef is one of the seven wonders of the natural world, Sofia took a lot of coaxing to join in the diving excursion, as it will mean getting her fur wet, and then it might go 'all massive and frizzy'.
Which would be a disaster, apparently.

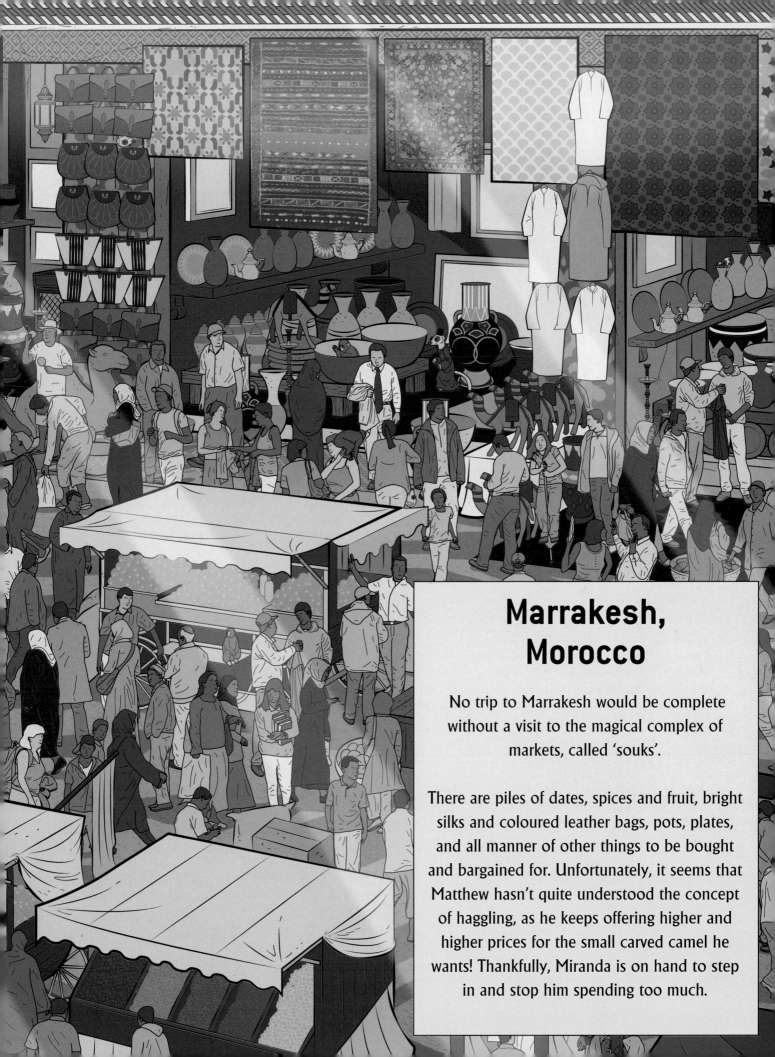

Marrakesh, Morocco

No trip to Marrakesh would be complete without a visit to the magical complex of markets, called 'souks'.

There are piles of dates, spices and fruit, bright silks and coloured leather bags, pots, plates, and all manner of other things to be bought and bargained for. Unfortunately, it seems that Matthew hasn't quite understood the concept of haggling, as he keeps offering higher and higher prices for the small carved camel he wants! Thankfully, Miranda is on hand to step in and stop him spending too much.

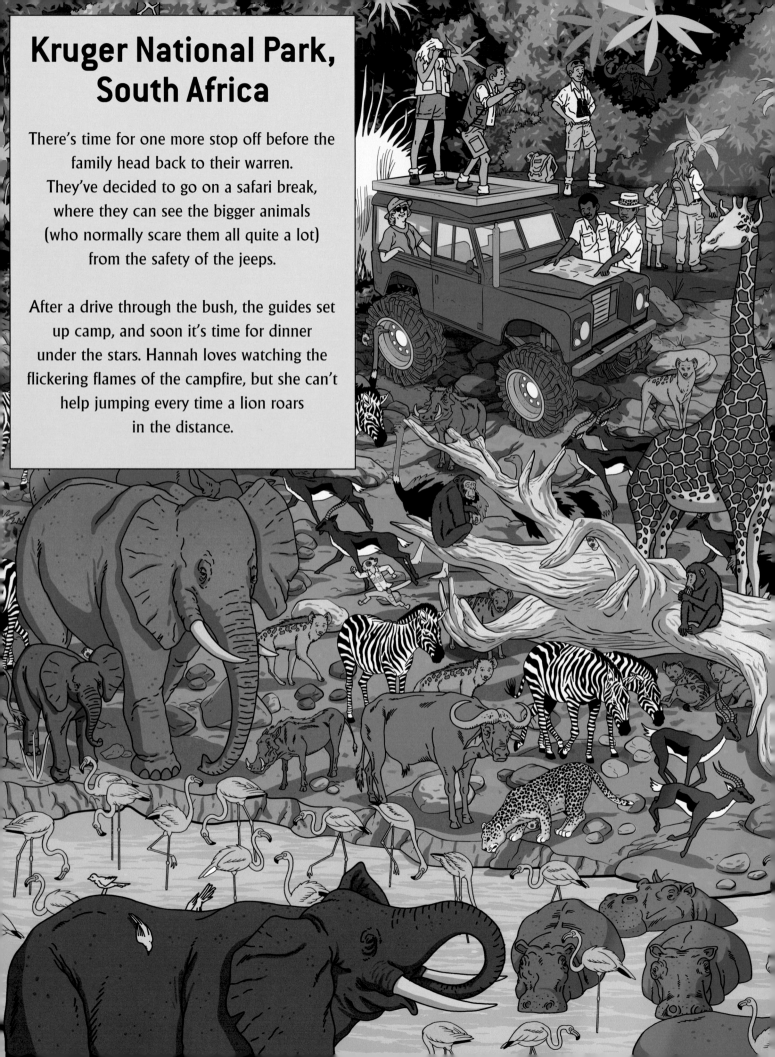

Kruger National Park, South Africa

There's time for one more stop off before the family head back to their warren. They've decided to go on a safari break, where they can see the bigger animals (who normally scare them all quite a lot) from the safety of the jeeps.

After a drive through the bush, the guides set up camp, and soon it's time for dinner under the stars. Hannah loves watching the flickering flames of the campfire, but she can't help jumping every time a lion roars in the distance.

Answers

Spotter's Checklist

A man in a green wig ☐

Sixteen blue balloons ☐

A tambourine ☐

A drummer ☐

A purple baseball cap ☐

Some tasselled trousers ☐

A polka dot bikini ☐

White elbow gloves ☐

An orange bag ☐

A dancer with mismatched shoes ☐

RIO DE JANEIRO, BRAZIL

NEW YORK, USA

Spotter's Checklist

Four taxis ☐

A clock ☐

A woman jogging ☐

A boy reading a map ☐

A man taking a photo ☐

A brown baseball cap ☐

A red sports car ☐

A police officer ☐

Some dropped litter ☐

A girl in a bobble hat ☐

INNSBRUCK, AUSTRIA

Spotter's Checklist

- Cups of coffee being spilt ☐
- A man eating a bag of doughnuts ☐
- Two alpine rescue doctors ☐
- A red and yellow snowboard ☐
- A man with a red bow tie ☐
- Someone relaxing on the ski lift ☐
- Some dangerous driving ☐
- A child learning to ski ☐
- A snowboarder with a goatee ☐
- A man getting his hat knocked off ☐

Spotter's Checklist

- A birthday cake ☐
- A cat among the pigeons ☐
- A man with a walking stick ☐
- A man on a laptop ☐
- A saxophone player ☐
- A woman eating crisps ☐
- A man with a purple briefcase ☐
- A lost boy with a map ☐
- An umbrella ☐
- A man sweeping ☐

PARIS, FRANCE

MOSCOW, RUSSIA

Spotter's Checklist

- A boy in a Jewish cap ☐
- A man reading the paper ☐
- A group of mobsters ☐
- A purse thief ☐
- A man in a bow tie ☐
- A woman with pink hair ☐
- A man waving ☐
- A group of nuns ☐
- A man holding a child ☐
- A man in ski goggles ☐

THE GREAT WALL, CHINA

Spotter's Checklist

Three men photographing the sunset ☐

A young skateboarder ☐

A man with a beard and moustache ☐

Two girls with fans ☐

A guard in pale grey ☐

A performance of sword Tai Chi ☐

Friends linking arms ☐

Someone wearing a purple beret ☐

A water bottle ☐

A man scratching his ear ☐

Spotter's Checklist

A romantic picnic for two ☐

An angry mother ☐

A stingray ☐

A pair of treasure hunters ☐

A game of cards ☐

A boy sucking his thumb ☐

An artist ☐

Men discussing the size of fish ☐

Someone who fell in a hole ☐

A man reading ☐

EASTER ISLAND, SOUTH PACIFIC

SYDNEY, AUSTRALIA

Spotter's Checklist

A baby in a sling ☐

Two space hoppers ☐

A bowler hat ☐

A red umbrella ☐

Two didgeridoos ☐

A barefoot person ☐

A man wearing shades at night ☐

Two ladies wearing the same dress ☐

A break dancer ☐

A pink headscarf ☐

LONDON, UK

Spotter's Checklist

- A news reporter ☐
- A blue trumpet ☐
- A lost camera ☐
- A guard in the wrong trousers ☐
- A man hugging his daughter ☐
- A girl sucking her thumb ☐
- Three Union Jack flags ☐
- A sunburnt man ☐
- Some stripy trousers ☐
- A broken lamppost ☐

Spotter's Checklist

- A monk ☐
- A man with mismatched shoes ☐
- A pink and red umbrella ☐
- A violinist ☐
- A polka dot tie ☐
- One yellow sleeve ☐
- Four couples holding hands ☐
- Two gold masks ☐
- A girl in purple waiting for her date ☐
- A waitress on her way home ☐

VENICE, ITALY

GIZA, EGYPT

Spotter's Checklist

- A boy with a finger trap ☐
- A modern-day pharoah ☐
- A man toppling over backwards ☐
- A boy with a tray of basboosa cakes ☐
- A man on his mobile phone ☐
- A girl putting her hair up ☐
- A man with a large cardboard box ☐
- A tiny mummy ☐
- A child on her mother's shoulders ☐
- A man in an orange cowboy hat ☐

Spotter's Checklist

BANGKOK, THAILAND

A pink hat	☐
A boat in trouble	☐
A woman with a red rucksack	☐
A man in a tie	☐
A seller wearing glasses	☐
A basket of fish	☐
A pink parasol	☐
Two Thai flags	☐
Bongo drums	☐
A man in midair	☐

Spotter's Checklist

A teddy bear	☐
A sumo wrestler signing autographs	☐
A man with green hair	☐
A stag	☐
A man with a video camera	☐
A couple checking their photos	☐
Schoolchildren with a samurai	☐
A woman searching in her bag	☐
A girl with a touch-screen phone	☐
A T-shirt with a target symbol on it	☐

KYOTO, JAPAN

SANTA CRUZ, USA

Spotter's Checklist

A yellow kite	☐
A bodybuilder	☐
A human pyramid	☐
A stray dog	☐
A man with a Frisbee	☐
A boy with turtle armbands	☐
A football	☐
Someone who can't swim	☐
A guitar jamming session	☐
A man carrying green shoes	☐

GREAT BARRIER REEF, AUSTRALIA

Spotter's Checklist

A pink lobster ☐

Two fish with big pink lips ☐

An ugly eel ☐

A jellyfish ☐

A swordfish ☐

A dawdling clown fish ☐

A red crab ☐

Seven fish with a diamond pattern ☐

A diver with a knife ☐

A pair of yellow flippers ☐

Spotter's Checklist

A girl on a pogo stick ☐

A woman with a blue suitcase ☐

A green flag ☐

A large, grey camel ☐

A couple arguing about a plate ☐

A girl stealing an orange ☐

A bookworm ☐

A snake charmer ☐

A pair of yellow slippers ☐

A man picking his nose ☐

MARRAKESH, MOROCCO

KRUGER NATIONAL PARK, SOUTH AFRICA

Spotter's Checklist

A baby elephant ☐

A shy buffalo ☐

A monkey tempted by sandwiches ☐

A leopard-print hat ☐

A lion terrifying tourists ☐

A woman in a stripy top ☐

Three warthogs ☐

A chimpanzee relaxing ☐

A flamingo with a white tail ☐

A thirsty predator ☐

Published in Great Britain in 2011 by Michael O'Mara Books Limited,
9 Lion Yard, Tremadoc Road, London SW4 7NQ

www.mombooks.com

A CIP catalogue record for this book is available from the British Library.

Hardback ISBN: 978-1-84317-710-4
Paperback ISBN: 978-1-84317-711-1

1 3 5 7 9 10 8 6 4 2

This book was printed in July 2011 by
Shenzhen Wing King Tong Paper Products Co., Ltd., Shenzhen, Guangdong, China

Papers used by Michael O'Mara Books are natural, recyclable products made from
wood grown in sustainable forests. The manufacturing processes conform to the
environmental regulations of the country of origin.